TIMOTHY K.

NEXT STEP

HOW TO START LIVING INTENTIONALLY AND
DISCOVER WHAT GOD REALLY WANTS FOR YOUR LIFE

Carpenter's Son Publishing

FAITH • SELF • FAMILY • LIFE'S WORK

I would like to thank my lovely wife, Jane, for all of her encouragement, feedback, and support for the many times she had to sit with me and hear me talk about Next Step.

"WHOEVER SOWS SPARINGLY WILL ALSO REAP SPARINGLY, AND WHOEVER SOWS BOUNTIFULLY WILL ALSO REAP BOUNTIFULLY. EACH ONE OF YOU SHOULD GIVE WHAT YOU HAVE DECIDED IN YOUR HEART TO GIVE, NOT RELUCTANTLY OR UNDER COMPULSION, FOR GOD LOVES A CHEERFUL GIVER. AND GOD IS ABLE TO BLESS YOU ABUNDANTLY, SO THAT IN ALL THINGS AT ALL TIMES, HAVING ALL THAT YOU NEED, WILL ABOUND IN EVERY GOOD WORK,"
—2 CORINTHIANS 9:6-8

Introduction

Are you ready for your miracle?

If you're looking for balance and order in your life and want to achieve all that God has planned for your life, this book is for you. It's about faith but, it's also about action.

You might have faith, for instance, but why aren't you seeing the results you want in life? Because faith ties to action. When I was in the process of writing this book, I heard a pastor say that you can't sit on the couch and wait for God. And it's true! How many times have you heard Christians say that they're "waiting on God," and then years go by, and they still haven't achieved what they want. ***You've got to live up to your end of the deal, and go in the direction you're called. That's when the miracle is going to happen.***

Over the past thirty years, I have developed a system to put my life on the rails and

keep me laser focused. I realized early on that it was important to live with integrity, with God at the center of everything. When I was 16 years old, I had a wife and a child, and we lived on welfare and food stamps. I worked seven days a week, from before dawn to late into the evenings. My focus was to provide for my new family.

One day, my brother Patrick gave me a video of *The Miracle Man*, a movie about a man who overcame extreme physical and emotional adversity after a plane crash. I started watching it every day and began to see a system to the way life can be. In the story, as in life, faith was key to success. In later years, I read Tony Robbins' books *Unlimited Power* and *Awaken the Giant Within,* and both helped transform my thinking.

I developed an unshakeable faith and belief system, and in later years, I joined a men's Bible study at Willow Creek Community Church in Huntley, Illinois, lead by Craig Springer. We did two different study groups: first was the books of the Bible and then Andy Stanley's *Starting Point.*

YOU'VE GOT TO LIVE UP TO YOUR END OF THE DEAL AND GO IN THE DIRECTION YOU'RE CALLED. THAT'S WHEN THE MIRACLE IS GOING TO HAPPEN.

Craig Springer was so inspiring. He led each section with the theme that we each have a story to our life, just as Jesus does. It inspired me to take people to the next step, and I was so moved by the Holy Spirit that I made a promise to myself to get baptized as an adult, even though I was baptized as a child. My parents led me to God, and I thank them so much for that. I just knew I wanted to get baptized as an adult, so when the time came to sign up, I told Craig right away. Then he asked if I would tell my story and participate in the video that was going to be shown at the church service the day of the baptism. All the men in my Bible study were asked to share their stories, and it was amazing (Dennis, Mike, Doug, Brian, Jeff, Dean).

I knew I had to tell my story and share the system that God has placed in my heart. I had to share it with the world. So I created the *Next Step* Study Guide. This guide focuses on the four key areas of your life: Faith, Self, Family, and your Life's Work.

In the pages that follow, you'll read more than a book. This is a life tool for you to take with you wherever you go. What's your calling? What do the next ten years look like for you, your relationship with God, and your family?

There are two key triggers I've identified in my thirty years of teaching others how to set and achieve goals. First is that fear comes before confidence, and second is that you won't necessarily know HOW to do something you decide you want to do. Those two triggers are big distinctions.

Fear is a normal part of life; in fact, it's a survival mechanism. All those people who tell you to avoid fear are wrong because fear is just a God-given emotion, like joy, love, and excitement. Fear is in every human the same way blood and DNA is in every human. So you've got to be willing to take the next step. There's a mechanism in the human central nervous system that recognizes fear before it recognizes confidence. You've got to embrace a little fear before you become as confident as you need to be.

Overcoming adversity is a challenge, but the adversity itself is a tool to sharpen you.

As you read this book, you'll be asked to complete what I call a "Lifeline."

Life is a progression, and you're here to express who you are and be whom God created you to be. What does the future hold? Some people never know because they remain stuck in their comfort zone. I created a Lifeline Goal-Setting Plan that begins with today. I first ask an individual, "How old are you?" I next ask them, "When will you die?" The gap between that is your Lifeline, or the time you have left here on Earth. When people look at life as "the amount of time I have here on Earth," they tend to start feeling uncomfortable.

When I take someone through this program, I guide them to complete a Time Snapshot of Your Week worksheet that defines exactly how they spend their time. How much time do you work, sleep, love, exercise, think, or give? Then we look at another page, entitled "Circle of Influences." What people are impacting your time? It might be your family, your coworkers, your friends, your exes, or your neighbors. Most people have very little time for themselves and others. We often find something or someone in their circle of influences that drains their time and energy.

Finally, there's a section for "Conversations with God." I encourage people to focus these conversations on four specific areas. Of course, you're already talking to God, but you just don't know it yet.

Work the steps in each section, and before long you'll live better, see more clearly, and set goals with God at the center. You'll be ignited to have conversations with God that will inspire your goals and dreams. At the end of this process, you'll be able to connect the dots between your time, your circle of influences, and your conversations with God. From there, you'll learn how to direct your life more effectively. I'll guide you to think through these worksheets and the four important categories of your life.

No matter where you are in your life, this book will help you become more confident in your dreams. Remember the life adversity I talked about earlier? Being a 16-year-old father was a challenge. But I grew from it, and today I own a company.

When I was 32 years old, I put a model of a Lear jet emblazoned with my company logo on my desk. People would walk into my office and see the jet and say, "What's that?"

"It's my jet," I'd reply. "I'm going to own it in ten years."

And I did.

But for ten years before that, people walked in and out of my office, picked up the jet, and asked me about it.

Visualization is a big part of seeing and then achieving your goal.

I'm a problem solver. Throughout life I've been able to identify solutions to people's problems. I listen to God and then teach people how to identify the link between their intention and the action steps they need to get there.

Turn the page, and let's do this together.

Contents

CONTENTS

The Four Pillars

FAITH

Without faith, you're hopeless. You don't have anything pulling you forward. Faith is a belief in the things you cannot see. It's God's love, a dream, or a goal.

SELF

Self is the individual person. Ego, you—the person you are. It's *you*. In this book we will explore and celebrate self, because it's whom God created you to be. You are the hands and feet of God.

FAMILY

This is your lifeline on Earth. The people who support you or surround you each day. They may live in your home, or out, but their opinions and actions impact your life. In a properly running family, God is at the center and any challenge is faced together, through Him. In a dysfunctional family, God is not in the midst of decisions, and breakdown comes as a result. Families survive and thrive through all things, together.

LIFE'S WORK

What's your calling? A lot of people struggle with this. Your calling is not necessarily your vocation.

This book will guide you to embark on the process of talking to God in order to know where you're supposed to be in life. God moves you in the directions He wants you to go. It might be different in every season and evolve as you go. Are you a worker or a manager or a boss? It might change in different seasons.

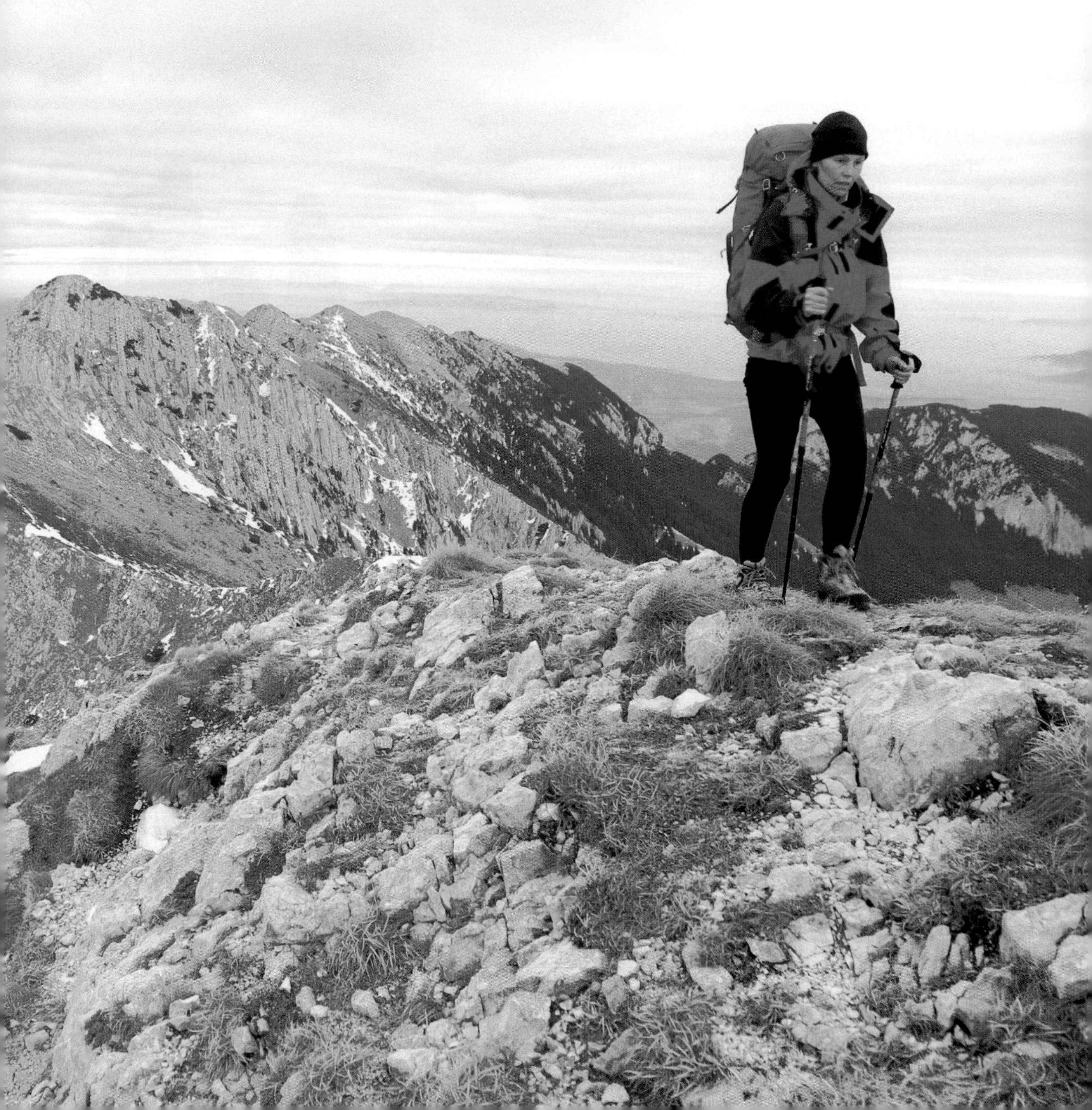

Instructions

SELF-STUDY:

Keep this workbook by your side as you navigate through life.

It's not just a book but a living tool that you can refer to, write in, and use to evaluate progress. As you read and complete the Time Snapshot, Circle of Influences, Lifeline and Conversations with God exercises, you will begin to feel a sense of direction and purpose. You can then define—and refine—your goals on your Lifeline Goal-Setting Seasons of Life Worksheet.

FACILITATORS' INSTRUCTIONS: SMALL-GROUP STUDY

If you're a leader of a small group, it's your role to facilitate conversation—to ignite and encourage God's presence in the individuals within the group—through the Time Snapshot, Circle of Influences, Lifeline, and Conversations with God pages. Lead people to have authentic conversations with God. As the leader of your small group, you will have a great opportunity to help others in their walk with the Lord. This will be a fun and engaging process throughout each session.

Journal Pages

JOURNAL PAGES

WHAT IS GOD TELLING YOU ABOUT THIS JOURNEY? TAKE A MOMENT TO THINK ABOUT WHAT YOU DESIRE TO LEARN AND UNDERSTAND FROM THIS BOOK. ASK GOD FOR WISDOM, AND WRITE YOUR ANSWER HERE:

_____

_____

_____

_____

_____

_____

_____

_____

_____

_____

_____

_____

_____

_____

_____

_____

_____

_____

I DESIRE TO LEARN:

_____
_____
_____
_____
_____
_____
_____
_____
_____
_____
_____
_____
_____
_____
_____
_____
_____
_____
_____
_____
_____
_____
_____
_____

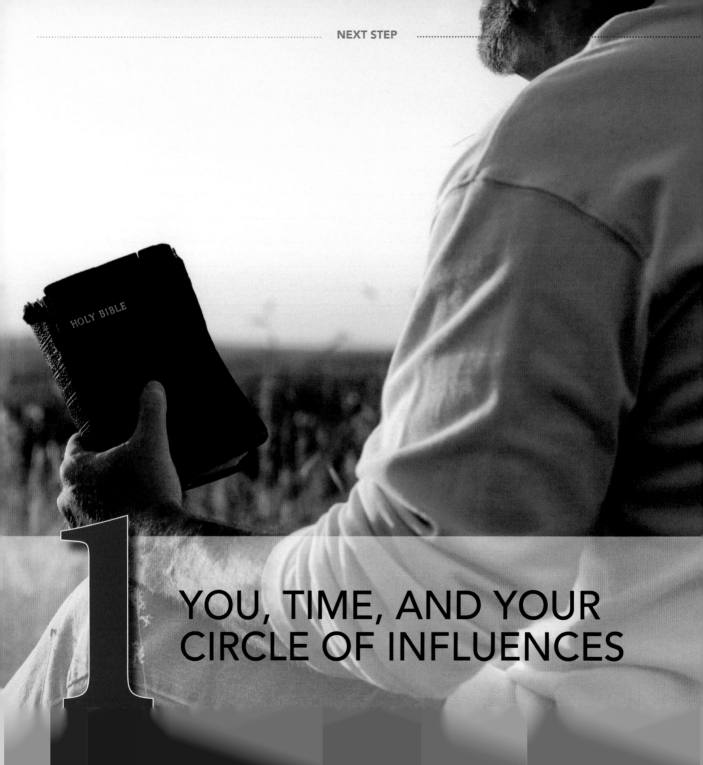

1 YOU, TIME, AND YOUR CIRCLE OF INFLUENCES

Who Are You?

In this section you're going to take a look at who you are (your identity), and what you spend your time on. Through this process, you'll begin to create more awareness about what's draining you, what's energizing you, and how you're living God's plan for your life. How do you keep all the dishes spinning? How do you juggle kids, work, family, health, and your life's calling as well as all the various contacts and acquaintances in your circle of influences?

KEEP THE DISHES SPINNING

This is about everything we do each and every day. Life is full, and sometimes, you can get overwhelmed. The more you live by God's word, the more you hear truth and get closer to God. And you know what?

Each day you start anew.

Do you wake up each morning fixed on Jesus? When you do, you've got a faith that you can tie into action. Start with faith, and connect the dots to what it is you want to do each day.

God created you in His image. Yet as we grow, and the world's opinions and experiences dilute that image and bombard us with other distorted and opposing images, it's easy to get lost. Some people get so far away from whom God created them to be that it becomes hard for them to find themselves.

Each and every day, we can start anew. All the good we sow will bring back good, and all the bad we sow will bring back bad, and those actions determine the balance of our life. The good will always overtake the bad. And when you stop the bad and sow both good intentions and actions, your life will take shape alongside God. Think of this as a partnership with God. This is a process of discovery, hearing Him, and living life according to His plan.

God created you to live here on Earth, over a fixed span of time. What will you do with it?

What have you done with your time so far?

Time

Think about this for a minute. Literally, give yourself one minute. God has given you time, which is one of His most amazing gifts to you. He can also take time away and bring you home whenever He wants to.

Close your eyes and think about what would happen if your time had run out—or if time was about to run out in a day, or a week, or a year.

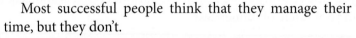

Most successful people think that they manage their time, but they don't.

You do not manage time; you can only manage yourself.

God manages time, and that's why it's important to listen to God to understand what God wants for you. Throughout this book you'll be introduced to a new concept called the Lifeline Worksheet. In a simple process of having a conversation with God, you'll be able to identify more clearly what God wants for your life each moment, each day, and each year. You will then place what God has put in your heart on your Lifeline Goal-Setting Worksheet.

What will that be?

Well, I can't tell you that. Only God knows. But if you ask and listen, He will surely reveal it to you. No doubt that God wants you to be His hands and feet, use your time for His kingdom to grow, and be a good witness. What does He specifically want for you in your life today? Where does He want you to invest your time and energy next week?

Before you complete the Lifeline Worksheet, it's important that you look at where you are now.

We will do a Time Snapshot of Your Week Worksheet that will show you where you spend your time. From this, you will ask God for help to use your time in the best way possible.

You will color one box for each hour you spend in each category, including sleep, self, family, and work, and you will use a different color for each category. Then you will add up all the hours in each color group to see what percentage of your time is spent in each category. So let's get started.

TIME SNAPSHOT OF YOUR WEEK

There are 168 hours in a seven-day week.

As you add up each color, place the total hours next to the color and divide it by 168 hours to get the percentage, or amount of time spent in that color (category).

This exercise will give you a new look at how you currently spend your time, and you

EXAMPLE:

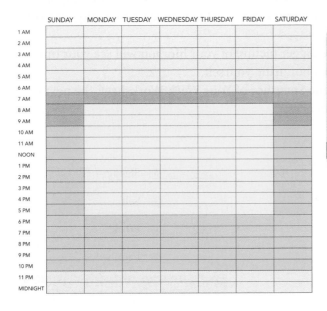

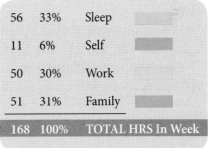

56	33%	Sleep
11	6%	Self
50	30%	Work
51	31%	Family
168	100%	TOTAL HRS In Week

will begin to reflect on how you use your time and see the balance—or imbalance—of your life.

For instance, how much value do you place on your health? If your exercise and health category is a minimal percent, but your belief system says it's a top value in your heart, there's a discrepancy. It's a valuable self-awareness process that will change your perspective.

In all of the time that I have spent doing this exercise with others, the one category that always stands out is self. Most people only spend about seven hours in this category, and that represents the time getting ready for work each day. One hour, each morning, for seven days.

No wonder we sometimes feel empty and lost!

Although we spend our entire lives with ourselves, we forget that we are in our body with ourself all of our life! The antidote is to listen to God, develop healthy habits each day, and re-emphasize that category remembering that you were created in His image.

I have found that people lose themselves fast with all of the clutter of daily living. Men become middle-aged and overweight; women get exhausted, unhealthy, and run-down.

When you focus on God and the bigger picture of your life, you will see your time in a different way. You'll be able to start honoring yourself.

Once you've completed your Time Snapshot of Your Week Worksheet, the next step is to think about your circle of influences.

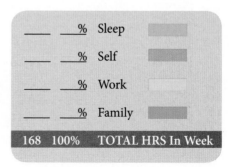

TIME SNAPSHOT OF YOUR WEEK

	SUNDAY	MONDAY	TUESDAY	WEDNESDAY	THURSDAY	FRIDAY	SATURDAY
1 AM							
2 AM							
3 AM							
4 AM							
5 AM							
6 AM							
7 AM							
8 AM							
9 AM							
10 AM							
11 AM							
NOON							
1 PM							
2 PM							
3 PM							
4 PM							
5 PM							
6 PM							
7 PM							
8 PM							
9 PM							
10 PM							
11 PM							
MIDNIGHT							

Circle of Influences

God wants to be your number one influence. He wants you to be in communion with Him. He then wants you to go out into the world to serve His people and your family. We all have a handful of influences that play a major role in our lives. The key to remaining in God's will is to learn how to manage your relationships and circle of influences, yet keep God as the number one influence in your life.

What happens when there's toxic or less than Godly influences in your life?

God will take you away from the bad influences in your life, and by identifying the

major influences in your life, you will learn to ask God for His grace in these areas. Each one of us has to make the choice to spend time with positive or negative influences. Examples of your circle of influences may be:

Grandparents: They are the leaders of your family if you were raised in a Godly environment. These individuals were here before you and have set the values for each generation to follow. As a child you loved them and looked up to them.

Parents: They are your first teachers. Their role in your life is pivotal because when they do not meet your expectations, your life falls apart fast. You then spend a large part of your life trying to put it back together.

Siblings: Are your best friends and can be your biggest enemies, too.

Spouse: Is the love of your life and the person you have decided to spend your life with.

Children: They are love and joy, not without challenge.

Ex-Spouse: This can be a source of a lot of pain in your life.

Stepchildren: Make for a blended family and can be a great joy and a real challenge.

Friends: Can help you in life! But the bad ones must go.

School: Classes can be fun, but the teachers can be good and bad.

Work: You will spend about 30 to 40 percent of your adult life here. You must feel that it is your passion, or you will not be happy.

Government: We live in a great country with law and justice, which provides us a strong foundation in our lives.

God: The joy to believe in God is your biggest source of peace in life.

CIRCLE OF INFLUENCES WORKSHEET

List all of the people and things you must deal with in your life:

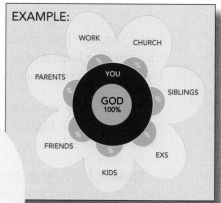

EXAMPLE:

WORK CHURCH
PARENTS YOU SIBLINGS
GOD 100%
FRIENDS EXS
KIDS

YOU

GOD 100%

Journal Pages

WHAT'S GOD TELLING YOU?

_____
_____
_____
_____
_____
_____
_____
_____
_____
_____
_____
_____
_____
_____
_____
_____
_____
_____

FAITH 2

HE OPENED THE ROCK, AND THE WATERS
GUSHED OUT; IT RAN IN THE DRY PLACES,
LIKE A RIVER.

–PSALM 105:41

What is Faith?

WHAT IS FAITH?

What is faith? Chances are you've experienced it at one point or another when, due to a lack of control or knowledge about a situation in your life, you've had to rely on God. That's when true faith kicks in because you've got to trust and believe that everything will be all right.

Faith is to believe in something you cannot verify, whether it's God, love, a dream, or a goal. It's the power we need to go through this uncertain life in order to carry on.

When you have faith you understand that God is the power of the universe; all good things come from Him, and your faith grows as part of that. When you have faith you can do all things through God.

EXAMPLES OF FAITH

God asks us to love one another, yet this is a very hard thing for all of us to do. We all have so many thoughts and feelings about how we are treated, and we often use this to determine how we will react to others. But when you have faith and work to develop it, you can let God guide you in this area.

God has given us everything we need and have. How often do we stop and think about all the good that is in our life? Maybe you express gratitude on a daily basis, or maybe you don't, but this section is designed to promote your awareness about this area of your life.

God gave to each of us the land filled with milk and honey. Do we know what that means, or do we just move through life without going too deep?

God has spoken to us and asked us to follow His word, but at times, we need to simplify things and get to the true meaning of what is being asked of us. If you're hearing God clearly, you are able to hear His instructions for your life. Taking action on the instruction is the next step.

This is not as hard as we make it out to be. It just has to occur one thought—indeed, one step— at a time, because our actions help us to differentiate good from bad. At the very moment we do something bad, we move away from God's truth. Most times, we intrinsically know this in our hearts.

God gives each of us His plan for our life. But do we listen? Or do we say, "I don't understand," and make light of it and not hold ourselves accountable?

Faith with no action is not what God had in mind!

God wants you to do your part, so you must get up and move in the direction God has placed on your heart.

Faith is not only reserved for God. There are a lot of areas in your life in which faith will help you. In fact, you may already use faith (and a belief that things will work out) as a way of looking at life. So keep your faith in close sight, and do not lose it when things don't go the way you want them to. Look to the big picture that God has placed on your heart.

Journal Pages

WHAT'S GOD TELLING YOU?

_____

_____

_____

_____

_____

_____

_____

_____

_____

_____

_____

_____

_____

_____

_____

_____

_____

3

SELF

YOUR WORD IS A LAMP FOR MY FEET, A LIGHT ON MY PATH.
–PSALM 119:105

Self

This section covers the concept of self, identity, ego, you, and all that God created you to be. Your "self" is the mix of mind, body, and spirit as well as a mixture of the world's views and life experiences. Self can be defined as the individual person, body, spirit, mind, and ego. (You and only you!)

This is where all reason comes from. We are created in God's image, and our body is the temple of the Holy Spirit. When you believe this, you will start to take care of yourself, and to take care of yourself is the most basic thing in life you can do. How do you take care of yourself?

If you don't know, now is the time to think about it.

You start with you.

You were created in the image of God. So that means it's especially important to take care of yourself, right?

Then, as you master yourself, you can fully move out from there into the world to express yourself the way God intended you to. When we take impeccable care of ourselves, we are giving the highest respect to God.

This is your number one responsibility, because you were created for the gift of life that He has given you.

So what about if you neglect yourself? Some people fall into drugs, addiction, overeating, and a downward spiral of unhealthy habits. If this sounds familiar, it's time to make a change. Not taking care of yourself is a sin of the highest degree.

You may have heard God's statement to sow and you shall reap. When I think of this, I see so much for us to be aware of, because everything we do is planting a seed (sowing), and even your thoughts, and of course, your actions, matter.

What do you sow?

Do you have a servant's heart?

Every day of life we must be aware of the truth we want to put out in to the world. Time is limited, and wouldn't it be great if we could do all the good we can, and always try to speak and do what is true and right and noble, and what God instructs us to do?

When you do this, you will reap a harvest of the truth, and your life will be in line with God's word. All the blessings that God has promised will come your way. Take care of yourself. This includes your mind, body, and spirit.

Another important consideration is belief.

What you believe will come into your mind and settle into your heart. It impacts all you do.

Belief is the most powerful force there is in our human experience, and with it, you can will yourself to die or will yourself to do anything whatsoever. The very thing you believe in is what your whole being will follow—from the smallest thing (like when you

should wake up) to the way you will handle the obstacles that come at you throughout the day.

Beliefs are so powerful that you will follow your belief, right or wrong. This is why it's so important to have accurate beliefs rooted in biblical truth.

> ## ABOVE ALL ELSE, GUARD YOUR HEART, FOR EVERYTHING YOU DO FLOWS FROM IT.
> ### –PROVERBS 4:23

I believe that God said to guard your heart to protect your beliefs, your actions, and your calling.

After all, if you don't believe in what's right, how can you live out your calling?

If we truly get in touch with this, we can direct our life in the way we want it to travel. We can work to change our belief systems to move our life in the direction we want it to go. All it takes is the smallest kernel of belief. From there, we can take it belief by belief to create the set of beliefs we want our lives to follow.

When we do this, we will become exactly the person we wish to be.

Unfortunately, our belief system is often on autopilot.

We sometimes do not pay very much attention to what we believe and then just react to life as it comes at us, one thing after another, all in one big maze of confusion! We live life without paying attention to what we really believe in.

The truth of life is what we should all be seeking. Your one and only truth comes from your belief in God (not just any God and not the universe), but the God of Abraham, the most high God—God the Father, the Son, and the Holy Spirit.

Now is the time to challenge your beliefs.

MAKE A LIST OF THE FIVE THINGS YOU BELIEVE IN MOST:

I BELIEVE THAT...
(EXAMPLE: ALL HUMANS ARE GOOD)

1 _____

2 _____

3 _____

4 _____

5 _____

FAMILY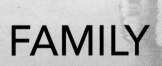

Family

What's your family dynamic? Is it strong? Large? Small? Nonexistent? Whether you have a family or not, God is still with you.

Family is the circle of love in human form that comes into your life. It's the individual human lives that you allow into your home, life, and inner circle.

It is so important to have a church family and friends that you can meet with and share your life with. The connection we have with people is a very healthy thing, but sometimes we feel isolated and disconnected; we end up pushing ourselves away from people and groups that could bless us even further. Why is that? Identify areas of your life in which you can build more connections. Once you do that, your life will take on a whole new shape.

Journal Page

WHO DO YOU CONSIDER FAMILY? IN WHAT WAY HAVE THEY IMPACTED YOUR LIFE?

_____

_____

_____

_____

_____

_____

_____

_____

_____

_____

_____

_____

_____

_____

_____

_____

_____

_____

Jesus had a family. Yet He also tapped His disciples to come into His inner circle and do His work. Who would you consider most like family among your inner circle of friends? These are the "3 a.m." friends you can call no matter what—you know they've got your back. They love you, they want to serve you, and they have your best interests in mind.

When God created Adam and said he needed a wife, the world changed. Husbands

and wives on Earth create a family with the supernatural authority to transform one another along with many other lives outside of the family. What goals do you and your family have? When you consider leading your spouse and loved ones and children to be servants to others in the kingdom, what do you think of? Take a moment to think of ways your family can impact others today.

Journal Pages

OUR FAMILY CAN IMPACT LIVES BY:

_____

_____

_____

_____

_____

_____

_____

_____

_____

_____

_____

_____

_____

_____

_____

_____

_____

_____

TIMOTHY K. LYNN

LIFE'S WORK 5

Life's Work

WHAT DO YOU DO AS YOUR LIFE'S WORK?

Everyone has a life. Then comes work.

Work is the expression of one's self for the purpose of income and self-gratification (Career, Parenting, Hobbies, Charities). Everyone needs something fulfilling to do that pays the bills. Yet sometimes, people confuse their life's work with their life's calling.

YOU IN MOTION

When you start out in life, the first thing that happens is you start to move.

A baby enters kicking and screaming, a curious little flurry of arms and legs and momentum. As we grow we learn to crawl, then walk, and then we begin to run through life.

And as you do this, you are alive, vibrant, and creating momentum in all you do! You think a thought and it creates a domino effect, and you exchange ideas with others and create. Life is a constant flow of momentum, and as we pour into another's life, it is reciprocated. Momentum is important. It drives you to your dreams. Without motion, there is no life.

As you develop and mature, there comes a time for income, and you then express yourself for income and self-gratification. We realize that money is the grease of life, because with it, things go a little smoother. For believers, money can support missions, build the kingdom, and transform lives.

Money is the exchange vehicle to acquire goods and services, food and shelter, and the items to help others, so to master how to gain money is essential to modern life.

Without money, you are dependent on someone that knows how to acquire money.

When you retire the income drops off, and you essentially go back to the beginning, where your expression is for self-gratification and fun. There's a progression in life as we go from student to teacher to mentor, and ultimately, to leader.

Think about this progression for a moment.

WHICH ONE ARE YOU?

Student
Teacher
Mentor
Leader

Maybe you're in the teacher stage, teaching what you know. Or maybe you're mentoring others fully, to become all they can be. If you haven't reached the level of leader yet, it's time to set your sights on it. Leaders share knowledge with the world around them, but they also create the platform to lead others. Leaders guide friends, family, and loved ones down the path of success, too.

WHO WERE YOUR TEACHERS?

Many people expect far too much from their first teachers. Unfortunately, when their teachers fall short in some way, they become bitter. They hold a grudge forever, which is a big waste of time! All you can do is learn from them—take the good and discard the bad—then move on with your life. That's how all teaching works!

WHO ARE YOUR MENTORS?

If you don't have at least three mentors, get them. Get one and two and three excellent role models to guide you in your life and career and faith.

People are a great source to learn from.

As a child you begin learning freely, because you understand that's what you're supposed to do. In class, your classmates learn the same thing at the same pace. But what happens as you grow older? Some people stop learning altogether.

WHO DO YOU WANT TO BE?

An employee, a manager, or a boss? A teacher or leader?

In life there's always a hierarchy.

An **employee** is a person that works for someone and is subordinate to their employer. Employees are expected to do as their employer asks, and they will be paid for their work.

What people need to understand is that when picking their job, there are only three types of jobs you will ever do: worker, manager, and boss. A **worker** is a person who uses both of their hands to do their job, so when you pick a worker job, you must understand that the kind of job you pick will determine your income and your lifestyle.

For example, if you decide to be a hair stylist, you know going in what the pay scale for that position will be. You can also determine what kind of house you can afford to live in, what kind of car you can afford to buy and drive, and how much money you will have to send your kids to college.

If, on the other hand, you become a brain surgeon, you know that your income will afford you a more opulent standard of living. But both positions are worker jobs, so when you stop working, your paycheck stops as well. That means you need to put money into a savings or investment account throughout your working years. This will help cushion the fall if you are let go or are unable to continue working for any reason.

A **manager** is a person who uses one hand to do his or her job and manages others to do the work. When you become a manager, you are leveraged against your workers. You can increase your income by how well you do at being a manager and by how many workers you manage. For example, you can manage a roofing crew of 5 workers or manage a nuclear power plant with 250 workers. Obviously, there will be difference in pay and the standard of living you will achieve as well as the lifestyle you will have. As a manager, the leverage is quite large. You could manage 2,000 workers or 10,000 workers, and the pay will be according to your managing ability. This has a lot to do with your personality to be a manager and you willingness to report to a boss.

A **boss** is a person who has decided to be a leader. This person has vision and the will to lead. Bosses are also the people who know they want to be in charge and have a passion for leadership.

But it's also safe to say we can all be leaders in life—in our families and in our peer groups. So what are the characteristics of a successful leader? When you look to Jesus as an example, you'll find wisdom, strength, and lots of conversations with God.

When you write out your conversations with God, you will start to feel a dialogue with God as to what He has in store for you.

This will change over time, or it may be a very strong calling, or pull, about what you are called to do. God wants you to express yourself to the fullest and do His will, not yours. God will be with you every step of the way, so you should enjoy it! This life is a gift *and* a journey.

So, again, let's examine a table about career choices, work, and salaries:

JOB:	PAY:	HOUSE:	CAR:	SAVINGS:	CHARITY:
Boss	475,000	600,000	60,000	50,000	47,500
Manager	125,000	295,000	35,000	15,000	12,500
Worker	65,000	165,000	21,000	8,000	6,500

By showing you this table, I hope to inspire you to think, *what is it I want to do?*

One option is to go it alone, as an entrepreneur.

Self-employment is one of the greatest things about America. It's also the way to express yourself to the fullest.

Free enterprise is a great opportunity to those called by God to this line of work, and owning a company can be one of the most amazing things a person can do!

LIFE'S WORK

People get confused about what their calling is. If you wash cars, it doesn't mean you're missing your "calling." Perhaps you're supposed to be washing cars, and you're exactly where God wants you to be. Maybe you're supposed to meet someone at the car wash and say something that changes their life. Maybe that's the place you're going to meet your spouse and start a family. Or maybe you hate the job you're in, but you learn humility or discipline. Either way, calling and vocation aren't always the same.

I love being an entrepreneur. But it's my calling. I love getting in the trenches, working my passion, and leading others.

You get to do what you love and hire the rest.

Most owners do not understand this, but it goes like this when you own a company: you get to pick the job you love to do and know God has called you to that position—and you get to be the best at that spot. I call this your "shot spot" because every time you get to that spot in your company, you do your best and love it! It's just like the final play in a basketball game.

As the owner, you get to hire the rest and place managers and workers in their own shot spot, then lead and mentor them to their own individual greatness.

GIVING

Giving back is the most important part of your life to love.

Do you have a servant's heart, or do you give begrudgingly?

As your life overflows with God's grace and abundance, you will become a conduit, and the flow of the Holy Spirit will pour out through you to help others. What and how much flows through you will build a life of love and opportunity that flows back to you, your family, and your business.

Open up your heart to God's children. Give back.

These chapters are designed to inspire you to think about your life. As you talk among your friends and family about these concepts, make any notes about what you feel or hear. What's God saying to you?

Journal Pages

WHAT'S GOD SAYING TO YOU?

_____
_____
_____
_____
_____
_____
_____
_____
_____
_____
_____
_____
_____
_____
_____
_____
_____
_____

TITHING

How much do you give?

Have ongoing conversations with God about what He has planned for you as His hands and feet, including just how much you should give back to His kingdom.

For example, everyone likes to think 10 percent is the magic number, but is that true? God will speak to your heart on this today. You may give back $20 and feel that is what God wants you to do, or you may give $20,000. Don't limit yourself.

LIFELINE GOAL-SETTING: WORKSHEETS (BY SEASONS)

Here you will write down the conversations you have with God. When you believe God has asked you to do a specific task, you will set goals in a time frame based on your age and season you are in. (Remember: God has given you a time frame for your life before you go to heaven, and only He knows when He will call you home.) Ask God for three goals in each of the four categories: Faith, Self, Family and Life's Work. Know that as you continue to have conversations with God, your goals may change. When that happens, simply update your worksheet with any new goals that God has placed on your heart.

This will put you on the rails, and like me, you will become laser focused. You will begin to have a direct connection with God, and the clutter in your life will start to fade away. You'll open a channel with God, and you will feel the presence of God with you all the time as you develop a direct relationship with Him.

After you have filled out the worksheet, you will then be able to see your life in terms of what God has placed on your heart. You will see the big picture that God has planned for your life. As you begin to feel a sense of direction from God, you will then move your actions in the direction that God has given. And when He alters your course (which He will), you will simply update your worksheet to again see the big picture.

I have done this for over thirty years now. God has spoken to me time and time again. I place what He asks of me on my worksheet, and it always gives me a solid sense of direction.

HERE'S HOW IT WORKS:

A lot of the time, people want to get all detailed in their need to know what to do in the next ten days, but that does not work for me. It is much too specific. I always wind up wrong. When you ask God for the big picture, you can work into it based on your age and seasons of your life.

For example, a lot of people go on a diet to lose ten pounds in twenty-one days. To me that is a big waste of time, and I would be surprised if God would ask you to do that.

God may view it this way: your body is the temple of the Holy Spirit, and out of respect, you should take great care of your body. After all, you are not respecting God by not taking care of His temple. I know this is not an easy thing to do, but when you ask God for His guidance—and you place it on your worksheet and pray over it—you will see God change your heart. When He does, you just may see yourself at the gym and loving every minute of it because God has changed your heart.

This will happen in all the areas of your life. For now, we want to focus on Faith, Self, Family, and Life's Work with only three sub-goals per category. This helps to reduce the clutter in your life since you are working with only four big goals and twelve small ones at any given time.

You may say, "Well, what about all the rest of my stuff?" Stuff it all into one of the twelve goals that have been placed on your heart by God (from your Conversations with God pages). As you do this, you will feel a huge load being lifted off your shoulders. Just give it up to God, but remember this: sometimes people give everything up to God and then they do nothing. That will not work because you must do your part! With this system, you will be following God's word directly through His conversations with you that you placed on your worksheet.

God wants you to understand the big picture and not get caught up in all the details, so look at your worksheet as often as necessary to stay on track and do God's will.

TIPS FOR COMPLETING YOUR LIFELINE AND CONVERSATIONS WITH GOD

1. When God speaks boldly to you and asks you to do great things (and have great things), place that conversation on your Lifeline Goal-Setting Worksheet.
2. God wants the best for you! Take action!

He also wants you to be an example of His word, so when you're tempted to say, "I should just wait and not mess up God's plan" stop it! You can't get in God's way. You can only get in your own way.

LIFELINE GOAL-SETTING WORKSHEET

Sometimes I hear believers say that they think that they are not allowed to set goals, and that we must wait on God. But this is not true! Ask for God's direction, and do it.

Below is a Lifeline Worksheet. I'm going to guide you through the process of setting achievable goals using the Holy Spirit as your guide. When God gives you the spirit to move on a goal, you should then do that by planting the seeds on your Lifeline Goal-Setting Worksheet.

LIFELINE WORKSHEET

As you write out your conversations with God, you will be validating each conversation. You will also begin to see a pattern in the way God is speaking to you and the direction He is asking you to go. You will then place these messages from God on your Lifeline Goal-Setting Worksheet. As you sow the seeds of your goals, you will begin to see your life take the shape that God has in mind for you. When God wants you to go in a different direction, He will speak to you. You will then write those revised goals down on your Conversations with God pages. Later, you can transfer this information to your Lifeline Goal-Setting Worksheet. Your goals will change

as God directs you, so you are never wrong. And, as your connection with God deepens, He will lead you through your toughest times to the truth of life—His word.

Everything you do and say is the sowing of your life as you develop a deeper relationship with God. When you have your conversations with God, He will speak to you. It is then your job to set a goal to fulfill God's message to you.

EXAMPLE:

YEAR:	2014	2015	2016	2017	2018	2020	2025	2030	2035	2040	2045	2055
AGE:	59	60	61	62	63	65	70	75	80	85	90	100
FAITH:												
1. Go to Church	X	X	X	X	X	X	X	X	X	X	X	X
2. Read the Bible	X	X	X	X	X	X	X	X	X	X	X	X
3. Go on Mission Trip		X				X						
SELF:												
1. Eat Great	X	X	X	X	X	X	X	X	X	X	X	X
2. Work Out	X	X	X	X	X	X	X	X	X	X	X	X
3. Fly Helicopters	X	X	X	X	X	X	X	X	X			
FAMILY:												
1. Wife and I Vacation	X	X	X	X	X	X	X	X	X	X	X	X
2. Family Vacations	X	X	X	X	X	X	X					
3. New Friends	X	X	X	X	X	X	X	X	X	X	X	X
LIFE'S WORK:												
1. Grow Company	X	X	X	X	X	X	X	X	X			
2. Write Books	X		X		X							
3. Give Back	X	X	X	X	X	X	X	X	X	X	X	X

LIFELINE GOAL-SETTING PLAN - SEASONS OF LIFE

YEAR:														CALLED HOME
AGE:														
FAITH:														
1.														
2.														
3.														
SELF:														
1.														
2.														
3.														
FAMILY:														
1.														
2.														
3.														
LIFE'S WORK:														
1.														
2.														
3.														

6 CONVERSATIONS WITH GOD

Conversations with God

HOW DO YOU TALK TO GOD?

This book will ignite you to have bold and meaningful talks with your Creator. Remember, He created you. There is nothing He cannot see.

As you walk with God, you will notice Him tugging on you, whereas in the past, you may not have noticed. These pages are for you to write down the conversations you have with God, and as you do, you will develop a comfortable dialogue with Him.

This may happen throughout the day or in the middle of the night. Regardless of when these conversations happen, it's important that you write everything down on your Conversations with God pages.

I have done this for over thirty years, and the connection this has given me with God is direct and instant. I have even gotten up in the middle of the night many times when things are weighing heavy on my mind. I have learned that this is natural.

Imagine what people are missing when they try to self-medicate with sleep medication or alcohol. They miss the chance to have meaningful conversations with God about whatever is worrying them in life.

When you learn to let God flow through you like a river, you will learn that sometimes the river will flow fast and sometimes slow and sometimes high and sometimes low.

So even if it's in the middle of the night, wake up and record your conversation with God. You'll then go back to bed and sleep like a baby!

Sometimes, when I have a lot on my mind and cannot fall asleep, I lay on my back and fold my hands and say to God, "I would like to go to sleep, so when You're done, please let me, because I have to get up early in the morning!" When I give it up to God, I am asleep in no time. This has worked for me for a long time.

Conversations with God

WHAT'S GOD SAYING TO YOU? USE THIS SECTION AS A NOTEBOOK TO MAKE A COMPLETE RECORD OF YOUR CONVERSATIONS WITH GOD:

RESOURCES

TIME SNAPSHOT OF YOUR WEEK

	SUNDAY	MONDAY	TUESDAY	WEDNESDAY	THURSDAY	FRIDAY	SATURDAY
1 AM							
2 AM							
3 AM							
4 AM							
5 AM							
6 AM							
7 AM							
8 AM							
9 AM							
10 AM							
11 AM							
NOON							
1 PM							
2 PM							
3 PM							
4 PM							
5 PM							
6 PM							
7 PM							
8 PM							
9 PM							
10 PM							
11 PM							
MIDNIGHT							

SLEEP	SELF	WORK	FAMILY		
____ hrs ____ %	____ hrs ____ %	____ hrs ____ %	____ hrs ____ %	168 hrs	100% TOTAL In Week

TIME SNAPSHOT OF YOUR WEEK

	SUNDAY	MONDAY	TUESDAY	WEDNESDAY	THURSDAY	FRIDAY	SATURDAY
1 AM							
2 AM							
3 AM							
4 AM							
5 AM							
6 AM							
7 AM							
8 AM							
9 AM							
10 AM							
11 AM							
NOON							
1 PM							
2 PM							
3 PM							
4 PM							
5 PM							
6 PM							
7 PM							
8 PM							
9 PM							
10 PM							
11 PM							
MIDNIGHT							

SLEEP	SELF	WORK	FAMILY		
___ hrs ___ %	___ hrs ___ %	___ hrs ___ %	___ hrs ___ %	168 hrs	100% TOTAL In Week

TIME SNAPSHOT OF YOUR WEEK

	SUNDAY	MONDAY	TUESDAY	WEDNESDAY	THURSDAY	FRIDAY	SATURDAY
1 AM							
2 AM							
3 AM							
4 AM							
5 AM							
6 AM							
7 AM							
8 AM							
9 AM							
10 AM							
11 AM							
NOON							
1 PM							
2 PM							
3 PM							
4 PM							
5 PM							
6 PM							
7 PM							
8 PM							
9 PM							
10 PM							
11 PM							
MIDNIGHT							

SLEEP	SELF	WORK	FAMILY		
_____ hrs _____ %	_____ hrs _____%	_____ hrs _____ %	_____ hrs _____%	168 hrs	100% TOTAL In Week

TIME SNAPSHOT OF YOUR WEEK

	SUNDAY	MONDAY	TUESDAY	WEDNESDAY	THURSDAY	FRIDAY	SATURDAY
1 AM							
2 AM							
3 AM							
4 AM							
5 AM							
6 AM							
7 AM							
8 AM							
9 AM							
10 AM							
11 AM							
NOON							
1 PM							
2 PM							
3 PM							
4 PM							
5 PM							
6 PM							
7 PM							
8 PM							
9 PM							
10 PM							
11 PM							
MIDNIGHT							

SLEEP ____ hrs ____ %   **SELF** ____ hrs ____ %   **WORK** ____ hrs ____ %   **FAMILY** ____ hrs ____ %   **168 hrs   100%   TOTAL In Week**

TIME SNAPSHOT OF YOUR WEEK

	SUNDAY	MONDAY	TUESDAY	WEDNESDAY	THURSDAY	FRIDAY	SATURDAY
1 AM							
2 AM							
3 AM							
4 AM							
5 AM							
6 AM							
7 AM							
8 AM							
9 AM							
10 AM							
11 AM							
NOON							
1 PM							
2 PM							
3 PM							
4 PM							
5 PM							
6 PM							
7 PM							
8 PM							
9 PM							
10 PM							
11 PM							
MIDNIGHT							

SLEEP	SELF	WORK	FAMILY		
____ hrs ____ %	____ hrs ____ %	____ hrs ____ %	____ hrs ____ %	**168 hrs**	**100%** TOTAL In Week

CIRCLE OF INFLUENCES WORKSHEET

List all of the people and things you must deal with in your life:

CIRCLE OF INFLUENCES WORKSHEET

List all of the people and things you must deal with in your life:

CIRCLE OF INFLUENCES WORKSHEET

List all of the people and things you must deal with in your life:

CIRCLE OF INFLUENCES WORKSHEET

List all of the people and things you must deal with in your life:

CIRCLE OF INFLUENCES WORKSHEET

List all of the people and things you must deal with in your life:

LIFELINE GOAL-SETTING PLAN - SEASONS OF LIFE

YEAR:													CALLED HOME
AGE:													
FAITH:													
1.													
2.													
3.													
SELF:													
1.													
2.													
3.													
FAMILY:													
1.													
2.													
3.													
LIFE'S WORK:													
1.													
2.													
3.													

LIFELINE GOAL-SETTING PLAN - SEASONS OF LIFE

YEAR:												CALLED HOME
AGE:												
FAITH:												
1.												
2.												
3.												
SELF:												
1.												
2.												
3.												
FAMILY:												
1.												
2.												
3.												
LIFE'S WORK:												
1.												
2.												
3.												

LIFELINE GOAL-SETTING PLAN - SEASONS OF LIFE

YEAR:													CALLED HOME
AGE:													
FAITH:													
1.													
2.													
3.													
SELF:													
1.													
2.													
3.													
FAMILY:													
1.													
2.													
3.													
LIFE'S WORK:													
1.													
2.													
3.													

LIFELINE GOAL-SETTING PLAN - SEASONS OF LIFE

YEAR:													CALLED HOME
AGE:													
FAITH:													
1.													
2.													
3.													
SELF:													
1.													
2.													
3.													
FAMILY:													
1.													
2.													
3.													
LIFE'S WORK:													
1.													
2.													
3.													

LIFELINE GOAL-SETTING PLAN - SEASONS OF LIFE

YEAR:												CALLED HOME
AGE:												
FAITH:												
1.												
2.												
3.												
SELF:												
1.												
2.												
3.												
FAMILY:												
1.												
2.												
3.												
LIFE'S WORK:												
1.												
2.												
3.												

AUTHOR BIOGRAPHY

At an early age, author Timothy K. Lynn found himself facing adult challenges: at sixteen, Lynn had a wife and child, had dropped out of school, was on welfare and food stamps, and was working seven days a week just to make ends meet. At 16, Lynn had a singular focus: providing for his new family. Realizing that faith was central to having—and executing—a meaningful life plan, Lynn, through God's grace, began to develop a system for keeping his life  on track and maintaining focus. Inspired by Andy Stanley's *Starting Point*, Lynn created a system centered on the four crucial components of Faith, Self, Family, and Life's Work. That system evolved into *Next Step*.

Born in Chicago, Illinois, Timothy K. Lynn is an entrepreneur, author, and teacher, but above all, he is a man of faith. He has used the Next Step system for over thirty years. The founder and chairman of a successful company, Lynn lives in the northwest suburbs of Chicago with his wife, Jane. He and Jane are blessed with a blended family of eight children and eight grandchildren.

ACKNOWLEDGEMENTS

I would like to thank all of the professionals that came together to make my dream come true. Your outstanding work will no doubt help me change many lives with my book, *Next Step*. Thank you so much.

Larry Carpenter is the president and CEO of Carpenter's Son Publishing. Since joining the book business in 1987, he has served as president of Spring Arbor, the largest Christian book distributor, and vice president of marketing for Thomas Nelson, the largest Christian publisher. After stepping down as president and publisher for Standard Publishing in 2010, he formed his own independent Christian publishing company, Carpenter's Son Publishing. He is proud to be associated with great Christian writers such as Tim Lynn.

Maryglenn McCombs is an independent book publicist based in Nashville, Tennessee. A graduate of Vanderbilt University, Maryglenn is a native of South Central Kentucky. She has worked in the book publishing industry for over twenty years.

Martijn van Tilborgh is an media entrepreneur and marketing strategist. He has worked and lived on three continents in different nations around the world. He is the author of several books, including *Chronicles of Reformation* and *Rivers from Eden*. Martijn established and owns several businesses including Kudu Publishing and Four Rivers Media (www.FourRiversMedia.com).

Suzanne Lawing is a freelance graphic designer with fifteen years experience. Based in Nashville, Tennessee, she is a graduate of Middle Tennesee State University.

Right-brained. That is a good description of **Dee Reinhardt.** If it has to do with creativity, she is all about that. When social media advanced into the marketplace, Dee embraced it with a passion. Dee is a Type-A personality, energetic, gregarious, an extrovert, a planner, and a leader. Her "right-brain" kicked in with social media to help her develop new ways to reach out, new avenues to explore, and new methods to exercise.

Dee became a social media specialist and is now the principal of her own company, Time2Mrkt, Inc., specializing in digital marketing. Dee loves to teach people how to fish, so it is only natural that she shares her knowledge with the community, teaching all of the social media platforms to business owners and community members. She helps small business and solopreneurs plan, create, implement, and train or maintain their social media platforms (www.linkedin.com/in/deereeinhardt).

Tammy Kling is a global bestselling author who specializes in books that change lives. Her TEDx talk, "Words are Currency," focuses on how your words can transform the lives of others. Tammy's books have been made into films, and she is the founder of the Homeless Writers Project ministry. Tammy has been featured on the *Discovery Channel, Dateline NBC,* Oprah radio, *The Wall Street Journal, Primetime,* and in many other media outlets. Virgin.com called her one of the world's top ghostwriters, and she's written 107 books for pastors, CEOs, and world changers.

Tammy's books are sold to publishers in Europe, Asia, and Latin America. Her books *The Compass* and *There's More to Life Than the Corner Office* are distributed worldwide (www.tammykling.com).

PHOTO ACKNOWLEDGEMENTS

Page 15 photo of hiker is Adam A. Hamilton, M.S.Ed.

Adam earned his master's degree in kinesiology from Northern Illinois University. He has nearly 10 years of experience working in the field of health and fitness. Adam is formerly a teacher at Northern Illinois University and McHenry County College.

Adam is the founder and proprietor of Lifestyle Fitness Institute. The company provides comprehensive lifestyle education, training, and coaching. Adam is skilled in teaching exercise and nutrition, applying behavioral and motivational strategies to apparently healthy individuals and those with medically controlled disease and health conditions to support clients in adopting and maintaining healthy lifestyle behaviors. Adam's approach is education-based and holistic and addresses the total health of each person. The institute focuses on four essential areas of fitness in one's lifestyle; Faith, Self, Family, and Life's Work (www.lifestylefitnessinstitute.com).

Page 19 photo is Reichen P. Dvorak, my grandson

Reichen is 7 years old and in first grade. This is one of the first photos of his new hobby, modeling.

Page 24 photo is Reichen P. and Radic A. Dvorak, my grandsons

Radic is 5 years old and in preschool. Both Reichen and Radic both love playing with their friends and enjoy a lot of different sports including gymnastics, roller blading, skiing, swimming, baseball, wrestling, and soccer.

Page 29 photo is Jane C. Lynn, my wife

Jane is a perfect example of self. A Godly woman who was taken from her mother at birth and put up for adoption, Jane is the loving mother of six children and two stepchildren. She is also the grandmother of three and five step-grandchildren. Today Jane is a stay-at-home Mom providing love and care for her family.